How To Get Your Wife Or Girlfriend To Want More Sex

(For Guys Who Are Dating Or In Relationships)

Published by

Dating To Relating, Inc.
4001 Kennett Pike #134-590
Wilmington DE 19807 USA

By Mr. L. Rx

INDEX

Preface………………………………………………………………………..2

How to Get More Sex - Introduction…………………………………....5

    The Turn Offs……………………………………………….……6

    Failure To Turn Her On………………………………….….. 8

Foreplay – What It Is And How To Do It…………………………….12

    Non-Verbal Foreplay…………………………………..…...15

        Body Language……………………………….…..17

        How to Dress………………………………….....19

        Non-Verbal Verbal Communications.......................20

        Reaching and Withdrawing……………………….20

    Romantic Ideas…………………………………………...21

Follow Through – Be Good In Bed…………………………………24

    How To Make Love To A Woman…………………………24

    Tantric Sex/ The Kama Sutra…………………………….27

    The TRIPLE WHAMMY!…………………………………29

After Play – A Little Known Secret …………………… ..……31

About The Author……………………………………………….32

Appendix A: Sex Training Books From Dating To Relating…....33

Appendix B: Other Books From Dating To Relating…………....36

Preface

The purpose of this book is to educate men how to get more sex out of their wife or girlfriend.

The bottom line is that women like sex just as much as men do. Any notion to the contrary is uneducated and inexperienced folly. Women probably don't "need" to have sex as frequently as men "need" to have sex. But their like of and enjoyment of sex is as great if not greater than men's.

If you know what you are doing it is not difficult to get someone who likes something to do it more frequently.

When a man isn't getting as much sex as he would like out of a wife or girlfriend, he most likely is doing something wrong.

I have talked to guys who tell me their wife or girlfriend doesn't like sex and only has sex with them once a month or so. Well, actually if that is the case, you are doing something terribly wrong. Your wife or girlfriend is upset with you for many reasons and denying you sex is just her way of telling you something is really wrong.

Even a woman that has a personality type with a low sex drive will have sex with you three or four times a week, if you do things properly. That should be your standard for an acceptable relationship – getting sex three or four times a week. Women with low sex drives will still have sex with you three or four times a week if you go about it right

A good relationship with a high sex drive will approach daily sex and sex multiple times daily.

My first marriage was a disaster. That woman never wanted to have sex with me.

She had some psychological problems but my immaturity and stupidity as a man didn't help anything. When I got out of that marriage, I had many, many relationships with women while I worked off the confusion of my prior marriage.

This multitude of sexual relationships with women taught me how to be an excellent lover.

That was 30 years ago, and I have never had a problem getting the maximum sex out of a low-sex-drive or high-sex-drive woman since then.

Why? Because, taught how to be a good lover by women, I learned how to treat a woman, how to put her in the mood for sex daily. I learned how to build up and create sexual desire throughout the day (rather than just suddenly demanding it in bed at night.) I learned how to put "pleasing her" (rather than pleasing myself as most men are bent to do) as my first goal in a love making session.

I learned how to understand a woman's body I learned how to give a woman an orgasm every time I made love to her. I learned several Tantric techniques that double the intensity of a woman's orgasm. I learned how to give women multiple orgasms (even those who didn't know or feel they could have them). I learned how to be romantic. I learned how to talk to her during lovemaking. I learned how to make a woman feel loved by "love making" rather than an object of my sexual desire.

And I am still learning. In recent years I have learned patience. There was a time after I became a skilled lover that I was not interested in any woman who was not as skilled as myself. In my search for a mate I wasted many good women that I felt were not sexually compatible.

In the last ten years or so, however, with the development of patience, I have begun to pay back womankind for those kindly women who taught me to be a good lover in the first place.

I have taught women who were not very experienced lovers to be great lovers. I have learned that spending six months to a year with even the most inexperienced woman could turn that woman into one of the best lovers I have ever had.

Is it worth it? Well, if that woman has other qualities that you like and you enjoy spending time with her for other reasons, yes it is definitely worth spending the time. You end up with a person that you like for a multitude of reasons including a good sexual relationship.

HOW TO USE THIS BOOK

This book was designed to be a complete guide in and of itself or to be used in conjunction with the DatingToRelating.com website where you can download or read some 500 pages of additional materials on the topic.)

There are five free compilation eBooks/eReports available on the website that are referred to in this book – "Foreplay," "Body Language," "500+ Romantic Dating and Relationship Ideas," "Tantric Sex" and "How To Find A Woman's G-spot." (Download instructions appear in the text of this book.)

These compilations eBooks have hundreds of articles written by many different authors on the topics referred to above. Now you will not necessarily have to read all of the materials in each book, just the materials that interest or pertain to you. Since the information is presented in short articles, this will make that task easier.

For those of you who may have read and applied "Dating To Relating – From A To Z", and are familiar with the other free and paid materials on the DatingToRelating.com web site, you may want to read through this book quickly.

This book will guide you through and organize the concepts that you need to apply to get more sex from your wife or girlfriend. And it will introduce you to a few new sexual techniques that I do not talk about anywhere else. Then you will want to delve into the free materials on the website to get specific ideas on what you can do to enhance your sexual attractiveness to your partner.

For those of you who have not read "Dating To Relating – From A To Z", don't worry. This book will catch you up on basic concepts from "Dating To Relating" that apply specifically to the topic of this book, then you too can delve into the free materials on the website to get specific ideas on what you can do to enhance your sexual attractiveness to your partner.

And if that is not enough, we of course have other ebooks on our DatingToRelating.com website that will also enhance the information in this book. "How To Give Any Woman Orgasms," "How To Make Sex Last Longer" "How To Be a Great Lover," "How To Be A Great Kisser" and the age old sex manual the "Kama Sutra."

Finally there is "Dating To Relating – from A to Z" which goes into a more comprehensive understanding of relationships and what to do to repair them maintain them, and create them. Sexual relationships usually won't last that long if your basic relationship factors are out.

So without further ado, from a guy who hasn't had any problem getting as much sex as he wants from his wife or girlfriends in the last 30 years, please read the following and apply it ALL and I guarantee you, you WILL GET MORE SEX from your wife or girlfriend.

Mr. L. Rx

How To Get More Sex - Introduction

The biggest complaint that guys in relationships have, is not getting enough sex from their wife or girlfriend.

In a recent AskMen.com poll 44% of men said (when asked about their overall sex life): "I wish I had sex more frequently."

On our website, DatingToRelating.com, in a poll of single men "How to Get Your Wife Or Girlfriend To Want More Sex" and "How To Get Sex More Often" were two of the books single men were most interested in reading.

Guys I've talked to sometimes think that women just aren't as sexual or into sex as much as guys.

My experience, however, has been to the contrary. Women are by far MORE sexual and enjoy sex much more than men do. Their orgasms typically last longer and as a group they are much more capable of multiple orgasms than men.

Yet, is very typical to hear a married guy complain that he only gets sex from his wife or girlfriend once a month. And of course it has been the subject of many a comedy on TV and in the movies.

So why is it if women are more sexual then men that men are the ones who are usually complaining about not getting enough sex.

The answer lies in two differences between men and women.

1) Women don't get physically turned on as easily as men. And conversely women get turned off more easily then men. So if a guy is not doing or saying the right things to his girl, she won't get turned on, and in fact might get turned off.

2) Combine this with the fact that women have one ability that men don't have and you will start to get a better understanding of the situation -- Even though women are more sexual and enjoy sex more deeply than men are capable of, women are also capable of going without sex for longer periods of time. Women are not as sexually "needy" as men.

Let's put it another way - Sex is first and foremost a "quality" thing for women.

Look at some of the women's complaints in polls:

> 90% of women reported that they wished their partner kissed them more or with more passion.

> 65% of women felt their partner did not have a good kissing technique.

So you see men are more into quantity and women are more into quality.

But, here is what you should know, if you give a woman the "quality" of sexual relations that she is desiring then she will want the quantity. And when you really turn your woman on, and she is in the quality and quantity mode. Most women will have most men on the mat screaming "No Mas" in a short period of time.

So if your woman is not having sex with you as frequently as you'd like, then you can safely assume that you are not doing something right in the "quality" department. You are either turning her off or not turning her on - in any case you are doing something wrong.

Now, what do guys do wrong to mess up the frequency of their sex life. Well there are probably 100s of answers to that one and millions of unique variations on the theme. But, here are some of the more basic and frequent mistakes that men make in their relationships with women.

The Turn Offs:

First let's look at what guys can do to turn women off.

1) Being a slob, smelly, or physically disgusting. - I don't think I have to go into this too much, but if you want sex, you might try approaching your woman when you are fresh and clean, rather than dirty and smelly. If you like to have sex when you go to bed at night, try taking a shower first. Make sure she knows you are doing that, then get romantic.

Pay attention to little details like figernails and toenalis and feet. Make sure your beard is not to rough. Some woman have deleicate skin and guys beards can scratch or hurt them.

2) Not taking care of your responsibilities as a man. - Most often it is not about being dirty and smelly but about not doing your job as a man. Men are supposed to support a family. They are supposed to take care of women. Although women are liberated these days and work and earn money like men, that doesn't mean that having to work and support a family turns them on. Most women are ok with contributing to the support of the family unit or boyfriend/girlfriend team, but when they start contributing more than the man and the man is plainly not doing his fair share because he is lazy or some such other trait, that's when women get a little turned off and resentful.

Almost every time I go out to a nice restaurant and I see a young couple paying for the meal, it is most often the woman that pays. What is that about? I can tell the difference between married couples and dating singles. Guys may think they are cool because their woman will pay for them everywhere they go, and they may even get normal sex for awhile, but I guarantee you women eventually get turned off by this kind of thing, especially when one of the girlfriends starts bragging about how well her husband or boyfriend is doing and how he does all these nice things for her.

Women can even tolerate a guy who isn't too bright and is trying as hard as he can. Women will even at times get fooled when they are young into thinking a guy has potential when he doesn't -- and thus they invest and give their all to the "rock star guitarist" who is trying to make his career. But that get's old after a while and after 2 or 3 years of that, women get turned off and resentful for supporting a man who is going nowhere. Women don't mind an equal partner, but they certainly do mind a guy who is just not being a man and taking on the responsibilities of "manhood" or making things go right in his own career.

3) Sometimes, it is not about career and the responsibilities of manhood , but about equality of effort and fair exchange amongst group members. So when the guy and the women both have jobs and the guy is holding his own and even making a little more than the woman, that is all good except when they both come home and she is expected to clean up the house and do his laundry while he sits around lazily and drinks beer.

You see, all of the above scenarios are mood killers for women. Even though women may tolerate some of these behaviors at first, in a long term relationship these kind of behaviors eventually catch up with her and start killing the mood.

4) On top of that is communication. Because of the above perceived inequities women will start "bitching' at men about their career or their responsibilities or their chores at home, etc. When men are unresponsive to communication, to discussing and handling the complaints, etc. there is only one direction for the communication to go - less sex. She is not turned on. She can't change anything about it with communication, so she just becomes not interested in sex . Some women may even consciously withhold sex on purpose to get across to you that "something is wrong" and that "we need to talk."

When a guy still doesn't get what this "lack of sexual interest" is really about, the relationship becomes doomed to one of mediocrity or eventual breakup.

5) Too much reach/not enough use of gradients – Now this is an interesting one and often overlooked. I go into the observation of motion and gradients extensively in "Dating To Relating.com – From A To Z." These are key topics to the understanding of seduction and creating successful relationships. For a full treatment of this topic you should review the information there.

But as a quick tutorial let take a look at what most of us understand – "clingy." No one likes a clingy person. You know someone who is always in your space following you around, has to be with you at all times. You know they sort of invade your personal space too much.

Well guys don't realize it but girls often view what guys see as affection and admiration and interest as an invasion of their personal space.

The whole point of observing motion is to observe what makes a person move toward you and what makes them move away from you. You want to do the things that make them move toward you and stop doing the things that make them move away from you.

The topic of seduction totally centers around the use of gradients and changing a persons behavior in small steps. When guys focus on "sex" too much and don't use the steps of the ladder leading up to sex (various levels of foreplay) they actually start turning woman off rather than on.

I can't stress how important this simple observation is in sexual relationships.

When you are constantly talking about sex, constantly touching a woman sexually, constantly insinuating sex without a reciprocal flow you are actually turning a woman off. Now everyone is different. So what is too much? Just observe the woman.

You want to attract and seduce a woman. If you are the one always calling her and she never calls you – you are doing something wrong. If you are always doing her favors and she never does anything for you – you are doing something wrong. If you are always talking about sex and she never brings it up – you are doing something wrong. If you are always reaching at her, grabbing her, touching her sexually and she doesn't reciprocate with like kind, you are doing something wrong. If you are always wanting sex, and she isn't. You are doing something wrong.

Often this can be corrected quite easily. Simply don't touch the woman as much, and do it in the right gradient. Don't grab her butt or breasts in a first attempt to turn her on – hold her hand. Do are say something romantic rather than sexual. Get the idea?

But remember every woman is a unique individual. Observe her, she will tell you what is the right amount of reach. If she is always pulling away and saying no to your sexual advances, you are turning her off. Stop doing those things. Try lower gradients of flirting, handholding, romance etc. and build it up slowly. Notice what makes her respond and reach toward you sexually. Do more of those things.

Failure To Turn Her On

I think the majority of "lack of sexual interest" exhibited by women are the result of the above mistakes - which really just turn women off sexually.

Occasionally however, it is not because of the above, it is because of a failure to turn women on properly, that sexual interest is lost.

Most commonly it is actually both things at once, because most men who are turning women off are simultaneously failing to turn them on. So most guys who are not getting sex often enough need to work both on turning women on as well as not turning women off . However, occasionally there are guys who are not turning women off, they just aren't doing a very good job at turning women on. That is an easier case to handle.

What mistakes do guys make in regards to turning women on? Here are the four most common mistakes that I find men making with respect to turning women on.

1) No Romance - Now I've talked about this one extensively in my other writings. So let me just put it simply here. You can't stop romancing a girl after you get her to be your girlfriend or wife. Whatever you did to get the girl, you have to keep doing it, do it more extensively, find new ways of doing it, etc. - as long as you want to keep creating a relationship with this person, you have to keep creating romance with them.

If you opened the door for her, bought her flowers, and watched chick movies with her to get her, you can't stop doing those things now that she is your girlfriend or wife. It won't work. Go back to doing whatever you did to get her in the first place and continue doing it forever.

If you don't like doing it then you made a foundational mistake in the firt place. Your relationship was built on a lie. NEVER DO OR SAY anthing you don't like to do or say to attract a woman. You are dooming the eventual relationship by attracting a woman that is not compatible to you with a lie.

There is someone for everyone, so however you are, tell the truth about it and attract a woman who is okay with that. That way you WILL be able to continue doing whatever it is you did to attract the woman in the first place the rest of your life.

2) Boring Sexual Routine - Sometimes people fall into a sexual routine that is fun a first put becomes boring when done day after day, night after night. Try some new things. Vary the routine. It will help keep things fresh and interesting between the two of you. Talk about your likes, desires, and new things you would like to try. Talk about your fantasies. Be willing to do things she would like to do, in exchange for trying things you would like to do. If you run out of ideas, we have several sex training eBooks on our website, "How To Be a Great Lover," "How To Be A Great Kisser," "The Kama Sutra," "Tantric Sex," "How To Find The G-spot," "How To Give Any Woman Orgasms," "How To Make Sex Last Longer," and other training materials to help you out with ideas.

3) Not understanding a woman's body - a lot of guys, especially the younger ones, don't understand a woman's body. Women need more preparatory (before actual sex) stimulation than men. Men only have to think about it and seem to be ready to do the deed. Women need to think about it and think about it and think about it to become interested and fully turned on.

Extensive foreplay is a necessity for women to get physically ready and mentally ready to enjoy and get into sex. Talking, having a romantic dinner, holding hands, kissing for hours (like you did on your first dates) all prepares a woman's body for sex and turns her on. Never, never, never try to have intercourse with a woman until she is turned on. Keep kissing, keep touching, but never have intercourse until she is totally turned on.

How do you know when she is totally turned on? Well, she will be soaking wet and she won't need any lubricant. Lubricant was invented because guys don't know how or don't take the time to turn a woman on. When you turn a woman on, you won't ever need lubricant.

4) Not taking a woman to orgasm and/or multiple orgasms. – In our sexually uneducated society, many women go years after their first sexual relationship before they actually have an orgasm. All women are capable of orgasm and practically any woman is capable of multiple orgasms. Many women think they aren't so they don't try orgasm or multiple orgasm, and many aren't turned on enough or are a little turned off by their lover so that prevents them from having orgasms and multiple orgasms.

And probably the biggest factor for younger women is that they don't have a partner experienced enough (the blind leading the blind) or considerate enough to learn how to bring them to orgasm or multiple orgasms.

In our society their have been debates for decades by so-called sex experts over whether women can have multiple orgasms or not. I never quite understood this debate as any experienced guy know that many women have multiple orgasms. And the reality is that practically all women CAN have multiple orgasms. Some need some time between orgasms, while others are little orgasmic machines that can continue having orgasm after orgasm for hours on end. The ability to orgasm and to have multiple orgasms can be developed in women who think they are incapable by a knowledgable man.

This is a subject that books are written on and if you don't know how to make a woman orgasm than I suggest you get one and learn how to make a woman orgasm. (See "How to Make Any Woman Orgasm" on our website.)

Making a woman multiple orgasm is similar. You need to learn to observe your partner's body. Learn and understand how it works. Some men are even unsure if a woman is even having an orgasm.

If you are observant you will start to observe and know when she is having an orgasm. Sometimes you can feel the orgasm tighten around you as you are having sex, other times you can feel the woman's whole body tighten as she begins to orgasm, sometimes there is quiver or a vibration from her as she begins to orgasm, other times she begins to get vocal as she orgasms, or the opposite, she becomes silent as she begins to orgasm

Each woman is uniquely different from my experiences, but any woman can be figured out if you just become observant.

Sometimes a woman's vagina gets sore or dry after the first orgasm and you need to withdraw from sexual intercourse after she orgasms and go back to light foreplay, building the foreplay up again into another orgasm later. Other women stay lubricated after the first orgasm and you can just continue having sex and the woman will orgasm over and over again.

As I have said, women are uniquely different and you will just need to observe your partner and figure out how to get her to multiple orgasm. As a general principle however, whenever it hurts her, back off of intercourse and go back to foreplay. Never have intercourse until she is naturally wet.

For some women multiple orgasms are achieved outside of intercourse. My last girlfriend liked to have the first orgasm by finger or hand, the second by mouth, and the third and subsequent orgasms by intercourse.

This may work well for a woman who becomes dry or irritated by intercourse after her first orgasm, but you can also do the reverse in that case, depending on the woman -- first orgasm by intercourse then second or third orgasm by mouth or hand.

For some women, orgasms are always achieved outside of intercourse. Sometimes two bodies just don't fit together the right way to naturally create an orgasm for the woman. Be willing to give your partner an orgasm each time you have sex, any way you can - by finger or hand, by mouth, or by machine if you have to.

Please your partner. Do whatever it takes. Always think of her and her pleasure first.
As a rule I always give my partner her orgasm or orgasms first before I orgasm as it is much harder (both physically and mentally) to give your partner an orgasm when you are flaccid.

If you learn to make a woman orgasm and multiple orgasm each time you have sex with her and you don't do the big mistakes to turn her off up above, I guarantee you she will give you all the sex you want.

I've even had relationships in which we totally did not get along, but the sex was so good for her, that she could not break up with me, and even after we did break up, she would keep coming back for sex.

In conclusion, if you learn to 1) NOT do the things that turn women off, and 2) do the things that turn women on, you will probably get more sex out of your woman than you can handle. Then I will have to answer your questions when you write to me like this:

> "My girl and I really have fantastic sex, and I really love her, but please, she is wearing me out, I can't keep up with her demands for sex. What do I do to slow her down, without offending her?"

Believe me guys. THIS is a reality!

FOREPLAY – What It Is and How To Do IT

A lot of guys think that of foreplay is having to kiss your girlfriend or wife before she lets you have intercourse. Well a lot of guys think they are great lovers, but a lot of women have other thoughts about that.... I have different thoughts about foreplay.

Foreplay, what is that? Good question.

Foreplay is whatever creates a little sex flow between your girl and you and holds it there in place so she and you can think about it and enjoy the build up and anticipation of what is eventually to come.

Another way of saying it is that foreplay is what "gets you or your partner ready" for the sex act. Since guys are just about biologically ready for the sex act "all the time." Guys seem to forget the value of foreplay, after all, it is something they have to do for someone else -- not themselves.

Bad way of looking at it. Why? Foreplay is not just for established couples already having sex. Foreplay is what prepares a woman to have sex with you. Hence, any woman you would like to have sex with that you are NOT having sex with would require foreplay.

So foreplay has a role in meeting women, attracting women, picking up women, dating women, having a relationship with women, and making love to women.

Flirting is foreplay....

I got married at 22 to my first girlfriend, and though I had sex for 5 or 6 years before we got divorced. I never actually made love until after I broke up with and divorced my wife. Why? We were both pretty inexperienced. Looking back, we had plenty of sex, but hardly any foreplay. The first time I actually made love, I was seduced. And there were hours and hours of foreplay.

So after getting divorced, I stood around bars and clubs nightly for a month or two. But after a while I started learning a few things. Then I started having sex daily (one night standers) with different woman. (This was the 70's -- free love -- pre-AIDS.) Man, did I get a lot of experience then. These women taught me stuff. Stuff, I didn't know, but now do.

One of the things I learned is that women like and need foreplay to enjoy sex. And surprisingly it made it a whole lot better for me too!

A Woman's, unlike a man's, sexual organ takes a while to physically respond to sexual stimuli and urges. Men can be ready in a minute, women take a little longer but mentally I think men and woman are more even. Foreplay can mentally prepare either sex in such a way to make the love making experience a whole lot better.

I feel that usually at least an hour of bedroom foreplay is a minimal amount of time to prepare a woman and myself both mentally and physically for the sex act.

But foreplay can go on longer than that....

The best kind of foreplay is Romance.... you know, shopping with your girl in the mall, holding hands as you walk, having a sexy conversation and flirtation at lunch. Little kisses and touches through out the day. Getting so turned on that you both can't wait to go home.

Foreplay can go on for hours and hours and hours.

When you are in the bedroom foreplay is kissing and kissing and kissing, touching, touching and touching. It can be role playing, talking about your fantasies, taking a bath or shower together, feeding each other, or watching sexy movies, or whatever other little sexy games you are into, if you are into that.

So how do you know when it is the right time to end the foreplay and start in on the sex act itself? Well when you are young and stupid, you don't think about any one but yourself. You start kissing your girl and a minute later you have an erection. Two minutes later you have her clothes off and you are trying to stick it in. Why? Because your thought is "If I'm feeling it, she must be feeling it too. See she's kissing me passionately isn't she. She must be feeling it." But, when you try to put it in, it won't go, so she offers to get out the old lubricant. She does and 10 minutes later it is all over. "I didn't have an orgasm she complains." "You want me to do something?" you ask, even though you are really no longer interested. "Never mind" she says.

It is a shame how many women out there have never been made love to properly. It is amazing how many women think that lubricant is normal, have never had a vaginal orgasm, or have never experienced multiple orgasms.

MEN, good sex for woman starts with FOREPLAY. Consider this your call to duty!

So, here are some basic principles for guys in relationships (if you want to know how to use foreplay to meet and attract and pick up women, see "Dating To Relating – From A To Z):

1) Always devote at least an hour to foreplay when you are in the bedroom. And use romance as foreplay throughout the week, days, and hours leading up to the bedroom. Women like to talk. Talking (and you listening) can be a very sexy foreplay for a woman.

2) Never, never, never, try to have intercourse with a woman until her private parts are soaking wet with anticipation. If she is not wet, she is not ready. She needs more foreplay. (And actually even if she is soaking wet, she probably still wants more.)

3) Always, always, always make sure your girl has an orgasm before you do. Why?

Because it is no fun having sex with someone who only takes care of themselves and then is too tired to do anything about you. If your girl has multiple orgasms then she might need to orgasm two, three or four times before you do. Not all women have multiple orgasms, but if you do your part right, most are capable of it.

Now these are generalizations, there are exceptions to the things I have written here. (For example, there is a small percentage of women who always need lubricant because of a medical condition.) But, if you know anything about my philosophy, from my other in depth writing, you know I am totally into situational technique. But the above is fairly consistent for about 80% of women I've experienced.

If you want some more suggestions for sexual foreplay techniques download a copy of our free eReport "Foreplay" at http://datingtorelating.com/foreplay.

Non-Verbal Foreplay

Verbalizing your sexual desire is not always the brightest thing for a guy to do. It works well when you girl is wanting sex as much as you do. But when you are wanting sex more then she is, you need to create a desire for sex non-verbally, before you verbalize your desire to have sex.

Why? Because it is a lower gradient.

Hell, I don't think you ever really have to ask a woman about having sex with you if you do it right. Sexual interest builds up gradiently. If you are observant you should know where you are on the sexual interest scale and what the next thing to do is.

What is the sexual interest gradient scale?   It goes like this:

Negative Sex talk
Then positive sexual talk.
Then Eye Contact
Then slight brief touching
Then extended touching.
Then kissing,
Petting,
Heavy petting,
Intercourse.

Now this is a scale I published in many of my writings, but it is a scale I also use mainly for woman that I am meeting and dating for the first time.

What about when you are in a relationship? Does this scale apply? When you are in a relationship the situation is slightly different from a guy trying to pick up a girl in a club or on the street, or a guy going out on a date, all to which the above scale applies.

When you are in a relationship, you already know that you can and will have sex with your girlfriend or wife (something you don't know when first meeting a girl). You have already been up and down this scale a bunch of times. The tendency for guys is to want to go directly to the last item on the scale – Intercourse – without stepping through the gradients. Many times women in relationships become guilty of this same tendency.

The problem is, that is not romantic. It will get old and boring (unless of course you are both totally and equally into creating at sexual intercourse technique - which is a different situation than we are talking about in this book.) very soon.

Remember what I said earlier. Whatever you did to get the girl you will have to continue to do to keep her. So the point is you have to go through these gradients leading up to intercourse each time you have intercourse. The gradients leading up to intercourse are sexual foreplay.

Negative Sex talk
Then positive sexual talk.
Then Eye Contact

Are usually first time gradients. Usually once you establish a relationship with someone they are not as important as they are when you first meet them.

So lets replace the first three gradients with TWO "couple" gradients.

Non-verbal flirtation.
Verbal flirtation.

And we get the sexual interest for couples scale

Non-verbal flirtation.
Verbal flirtation.
Then slight brief touching
Then extended touching.
Then kissing,
Petting,
Heavy petting,
Intercourse.

Remember our definition of foreplay above:

> Foreplay is whatever creates a little sex flow between your girl and you and holds it there in place so she and you can think about it and enjoy the build up and anticipation of what is eventually to come.

So when you want more sex from your wife or girlfriend because you are not getting enough, make sure you do all the basic stuff we have talked about so far in this book and stop trying to jump into sex at the higher gradients (Extended Touching and above) and start in at "Non-Verbal flirtation"

What is non-verbal flirtation. Well it can be a lot of things. But generally for men in relationships it involves:

1) Body Language – posture, stance, position, motion, etc.

2) Dress – from head to toes

3) Verbal communication not about sex

4) The motion of reaching and withdrawing

Let talk about each one of these a little:

1) Body Language – posture, stance, position, motion, etc.

Now there is lots written about using body language to attract women in general. In fact we have a free eBook on our website DatingToRealting.com which will give you a lot of information about using body language to attract women. (You can get your free copy here if you don't already have one: http://datingtorelating.com/bodylanguage)

I suggest you download it and read it. All of the kind of stuff talked about in the free eBook applies and can be used to a certain degree in relationships.

So smell good, look good, dress good, move good, etc.

Just because you got the woman you can't stop doing those things that men do in general to attract women.

These are all non-verbal flirtations and you have to do them with your wife or girlfriend just like you would do for some women you are meeting for the first time.

Smell good, look good, dress good, move good. These are general "turn ons" for a woman and will put her in the mood usually.

However, we are not talking about attracting woman we don't know with body language here, we are talking about using body language on someone who is already attracted to you to flirt with her and get her in the mood for sex.

How do the two differ? Well, for example, if you read the advice in the free eBook above you will see a lot of advice on using posture, body language etc. to portray confidence. Women in general are attracted to confidence in a man. However, our guiding principle with someone that you have already established a relationship with is **"keep doing whatever you did to attract the woman in the first place."**

Perhaps your woman is not like the average woman and likes shy guys. Perhaps she was attracted to you because you didn't portray confidence around women. Well if that is the case then flirting with your girlfriend or wife may be to go back to those non-verbal clues that you use to give off about your shyness and lack of confidence. Perhaps since you got your girl you are no longer shy and lack confidence with her and perhaps that is a "turn off" of "failure to turn on" for her.

Perhaps you have to go back to what worked in the beginning as a lower gradient each and every time you want to flirt with her or seduce her. Perhaps she likes it when you are shy and she originates sex with you. Perhaps you then can become aggressive and un-shy when you get to the higher stages of sexual interest such as heavy petting or intercourse. I do not know. This is an example. But go back to your exact overall pattern of how you attracted her in the first place, and exactly what you did at each stage. Maybe it took you

3 months to get up to intercourse and maybe you went from shy to aggressive in those three months or from aggressive to shy or whatever pattern you come up with upon observation of what you actually did.

The point is play out that same pattern of non-verbal flirtation and seduction each and every time you want to have sex with her and you just may find she is suddenly very interested in sex again.

This is not to say that a man can not become more attractive to a woman than he once was. So make sure that you are doing the things that worked and attracted the woman in the first place. Once that is totally in, you may review the things in the free eBook that are generally attractive to women. Try some of the ones you are not doing and see if it works for your girl. There is nothing wrong with making yourself more attractive.

There is also the fact that people change and grow. So perhaps you are doing the exact same things that attracted her in the first place but she has changed and those things no longer work. Well, first thing I'd do is communicate to her and find out where she is at. See how she feels about things currently. If you have been in a relationship for awhile she will probably have a set of grievances she will air.

Listen and learn. She will probably tell you what you need to do to be more attractive. If you still like and value her as a mate. Make the necessary changes.

Dating To Relating - from A to Z goes into creating relationships extensively. You may need to put the "create" back into a lackluster relationship. Try some of the body-language techniques in the free eBook to make yourself more attractive. You may need some romance. Read the section in this eBook on romantic ideas.

Another "body language" relationship problem is what does your body language say to others about your relationship? This too can be a turn off or a flirtatious turn on to your girl.

When you are out in public or when you or with either of your friends, what does your body language say? Does it say: This is my girl. She is the coolest most attractive woman I have ever known and I love her. (Probably a turn on); or does it say: I don't really like her, I don't want to be seen with her, I am embarrassed to be seen with her, etc.

Or does your body language say, I am a possessive jealous fool (something that may embarrass her in front of friends)

Walking in front of your girl (rather than holding her hand), not opening doors, sitting across from her in a restaurant (rather than sitting next to her), being obviously perturbed at her all the time (rather than obviously in admiration of her beauty) all give out non-verbal signals to those around you.
You see, being loved and admired in something we all like. Those that demonstrate that they love and admire us (especially in front of other people) tend to be a "turn on." Those

that make us look like fools, or stupid, or worthless to others, certainly aren't a turn on and are probably a turn off.

2) How To Dress – From head to toes

In the same free eBook ("Body Language" http://datingtorelating.com/bodylanguage) you will get some information on how to dress your self for meeting and attracting women. This data will also apply if you are in an existing relationship.

Women love men who dress nicely. It is a visual turn on for them. Would you like it if your girl didn't bother to get dressed up or look nice for you. No, you wouldn't. You might tolerate it – like she does, but you wouldn't like it.

Besides a visual turn on for a woman, a man who dresses nice for her all the time is an emotional turn on. It is another way of saying I love and care about you. It also gives your woman bragging rights in her locker room. It is something she can show off to her girlfriends and brag about how nice you are and what you do for her.

Now remember, that there are different women and different women like different things. So there is no universal right way to dress. If you want to be stylish, look at how men dress in movies, look at magazines, etc. look at girls' magazines and see how they like to dress up men in the ads in those magazines.

Ask your sister or girls who are friends to help you select clothes. Or ask them what they think looks cool. Look at popular guys you know and see how they dress. Consult guys you know who you know get a lot of girls and are sharp dressers.

If you want young girls you will have to dress one way. If you want older women you will dress another way. If you want classy beautiful women you should dress another way. If you want a middle class woman, well that will require a different way of dressing. Get it.

Dressing for women is another little non-verbal thing that flirts with her and just puts her more in the mood for sex.

The one thing that is different about dressing for women in general when you are trying to meet them and dressing for the woman with whom you have a relationship is that you can consult the woman with whom you have a relationship. Ask for her opinion. Ask her to help you buy clothes. Always dress the way that the woman you are with wants you to dress. THAT is what she is attracted to and what will turn her on.

It really doesn't matter what you think about it. Provided it doesn't interfere with your job or other areas of your life that require you to dress for success in a different way, ALWAYS dress the way your woman wants you to – that includes, facial hair, hair styles, and anything else you can think of that she wants you to wear.

But remember, just doing one of these things won't overcome deeper relationship problems. Do all the things outlined in this chapter and this book and I guarantee you will be getting way more sex than you can probably handle.

3) Non-Verbal Verbal communication.

Now this is an interesting one – using verbal communication non-verbally. What do I mean about this.

Well, for example, if the only time you really talk or listen to your girl is when you want to have sex. That says something to her. You don't care about her, you only care about sex.

But if you are willing to talk and listen to your girl anytime about anything, that means you care about her. And if you care about her, that means you love her. And that is sexy to her. And that will be a turn on to her.

So if you want more sex out of a girl show her that you care by talking and interacting with her in non-sexual ways. The more you interact with her non-sexually, the more you will be able to interact with her sexually.

So talk to your girl about all kinds of things. That is sexy. DO non-sexual things with her. Go to the mall, go shopping with her, be active - pick out clothes for her. ALL THIS kind of stuff is great flirtation time. It shows your girl you care. It is great foreplay.

4) The Motion of Reaching and Withdrawing.

I have been using the motion of reaching and withdrawing in a multitude of ways ever since I can remember as a foreplay and a sexual enhancement technique.

Now I talk about reaching and withdrawing extensively in "Dating To Relating – From A to Z." But as it applies to foreplay and sexual technique it is quite simple.

NEVER REACH, REACH, REACH!

What does that mean?

It means when you are flirting with a girl, flirt just a little then back off and talk about something else – non flirtations, non- sexual. Then go back to flirting, then withdraw again, etc.

Wherever you are at on that sexual interest scale - whether it is non-verbal flirtation, verbal flirtation, slight brief touching, extended touching, kissing, petting, heavy petting, or intercourse – always do it for awhile then withdraw and do something else, then go back, then withdraw, etc.

When you do this correctly you increase the intensity and desire for the action. This even applies sexually. To increase a woman's and my own orgasm (especially when I am having a long or all night session) I will have sex for awhile, then withdraw and talk about something else for awhile then go back to sex. I will repeat this cycle a few times and it will intensify the eventual orgasms when we have them.

You can do this a variety of ways. For example, you could withdraw from a certain sexual action without withdrawing from sex completely. – Kiss a girl for a while, then give her oral sex almost to the point of coming, then go back to kissing her, then go back to oral sex almost to the point of coming, then go back to kissing, etc. This will intensify her pleasure.

Get the idea?

When talking on the phone, talk for awhile then say "Listen I got to go. Let's talk later." Short little conversations through out the day are way more powerful than one long one. The reach and withdraw lets the woman know you are thinking about her all day and attracts her to you. Yet, she never gets her fill of you because you talk for a while and then you are gone. The whole thing is very powerful.

Touch a girl lightly when flirting, hold her hand for a while, then withdraw. This creates attraction. She want's more. She will be thinking about when you are going to touch her next. Touch a woman and don't let go and she will get tired of it sooner or later and wonder when you will let go or stop.

There are hundreds of ways you can apply reach and withdraw techniques. They are very powerful. Have fun using them!

Romantic Ideas

Romance is 100% foreplay. You can get lots of romantic ideas in my compilation "500+ Romantic Dating and Relationship Ideas" which you can download free at: http://datingtorelating.com/500romanticideas. With this eBook you will never run out of romantic ideas.

But let me address what romance is and how to come up with your own romantic ideas.

The dictionary gives us this definition of romantic:

Concerned with, or conducive to, romance and love; Idealistic yet impractical; Passionate and imaginative rather than structured

So how does one generate romantic ideas?
Let's take a look.

Concerned with, or conducive to, romance and love

Take your girl somewhere or do something that is concerned with romance and love:
A movie, a place, a poetry reading, a romantic vacation, etc…

Or read a book together, give her a massage, cook candlelight dinner, talk about first time you met, watch your wedding videos, dress up and stay home, play romantic music, read old love letters…

Idealistic yet impractical;

Play out her fantasy, rent her favorite car, surprise her for lunch at work, recreate first date, take her on a nighttime picnic, renew your vows, take her on a surprise vacation, name a star after her, take her on a second honeymoon

Passionate and imaginative rather than structured

Turn off the TV and play some romantic games, tell your girl 10 things you love about her, take a bath together, make a scrap book, burn a CD of her favorite songs, write her a love letter.

So we can use the dictionary definition to generate romantic ideas, but honestly, the dictionary often lets us down. It is easy to mess up on Romance if you do not temper it with observation.

You need to observe the individual you are romancing not just the idea.

One woman might consider it very romantic if you surprised her with a sky diving adventure or balloon ride. Another woman might get scared to death and consider you totally inconsiderate for trying to force something like that on her.

Most women might find "flowers" so, so romantic. But there a few who will lecture you that they don't like "dead things" and destroying nature and will tell you next time give them a plant.

So always temper your ideas with "observation." It is not romantic unless she considers it romantic.

Observation – One of the most romantic things you can do is pay attention to someone – it may not be that impractical and idealistic, but people lose romance in a relationship to the degree that communication and create go out. They do not loose romance because they aren't doing exciting impractical things. Relationships are built on the practical.

Relationships need the practical to define the "impractical." The spice and spikes of a relationship are the little creative passionate things you do to offset the practical. But without paying attention to the practical you won't know what to do that is creative and impractical.

So a few basic ways to be romantic with your girl are:

Show your girl that you are thinking of her.
Show your girl that you pay attention to her – the little things she says.
Show your girl you are always thinking of her.
Show your girl that you care

Showing someone that you pay attention to them and care is very romantic.

Ever been in a relationship and give your mate little hints about what you want for your birthday all year, only to have them say, "What do you want for your birthday. I don't have any idea." Not very romantic is it.

But if they are attentive and got your little hints here and there, well that is very romantic isn't it?

Always set aside time to be romantic and to pay attention to your girl. No matter how long you have been married or living together, you should always set aide one day a week to go out on a date and pay attention to each other.

So remember a truly romantic relationship will have a solid foundation of observation, good communication and the occasional impractical.

Do those things for people that they consider too impractical to do for themselves.

Buy those gifts for people that they want, but they would never buy for themselves

It is the thought that counts. Show someone that you are thinking about them and it is very romantic.

Now that you have some notion of how to create romantic ideas, take a look at our free eBook "500+ Romantic Dating and Relationship Ideas" which you can download free at: http://datingtorelating.com/500romanticideas, and use the ideas in this book and mix it with observation to create some romance for yourself and your girl.

Follow Through – Be Good In Bed –

Probably the most important thing regarding getting more sex from your wife or girlfriend is being good in the "love making" department. It does not mean you have to be this amazingly hung stud that can go all night long, etc. It means you have to be an attentive and considerate lover. It means you ALWAYS give your girl an orgasm, and make sex a very pleasurable and rewarding activity for her.

If you do all the things I have outlined in this eBook so far, you will probably get sex 3 or 4 times a week regardless of how good you are in bed. You will get it because your wife or girlfriend will consider you a good person and reward you for being a good husband or boyfriend even if sex is not all that rewarding for her.

However if you become a good lover, she will want it every day of the week and multiple times a day. As women get older they get more sexual and their sexual appetite increases, you will probably reach a point where you are the one saying "I have a headache."

How To Make Love To A Woman

On our website, we have detailed information on sexual technique. We even have mini-courses like: "How To Be A Great Lover" " How To Be A Great Kisser" and "Everything You Ever Wanted To Know About Sex Positions." And we have eBooks like "Kama Sutra" and "Tantric Sex." Sexual technique is again a topic worthy of a book and indeed many a book has been written on the subject.

But here I am going to give you some general pointers and an example. The example contains some basic principles even more basic then the techniques we have on the website.

Lovemaking is sensuality. It involves the whole body not just genitals.

Pre - Session

1) Foreplay - Foreplay begins way before the sex act and the love making session. Flirt with your woman all day and both of you will be real turned on when you are ready to engage.

2) Sobriety - I was 28 before I ever made love sober. Making love sober is a must. Alcohol makes a man slightly flaccid. If you don't believe me. Try it. Make love to your woman sober and inebriated. Ask her which one she likes best. If everything else is equal she will always pick sober over inebriated. Why? Because she will tell you, you are a lot harder when you are sober.

3) Cleanliness- Having been with a lot of women, it makes a big difference when someone is clean and smells nice. Keep your hygiene in. Take a shower; clean your teeth, use deodorant, gargle, etc.

Taking a shower together right before a lovemaking session can also be great foreplay.

Example of a sensual love making session your woman will enjoy.

1) Foreplay - now this is direct sexual foreplay - kissing, touching, petting, etc. You have to do foreplay for at least an hour. Touch, kiss, caress her entire body - not just the genitals. Women have many erogenous zones in addition to their breasts and their clitoris - Lips, scalp, hair, ears, neck, inner thighs, butt, and the back.

2) Every woman is different but I work my way up the erogenous zones. Start off with kissing the lips lightly and gently, work into making out with deep French kissing, massage the scalp and play with the hair while you are kissing her. Use your hands while kissing to tantalize her whole body. Play with her hands, her toes, lightly stroke her arms, her back. Withdraw from French kissing after doing it for a while (30-60 minutes) and begin to kiss her entire body with her clothes on. Talk to her occasionally as you kiss her. Whisper sweat nothings in her ear. Tell her how much you love her. Tell her how beautiful she is to you. (Keep the light talking going throughout your love making session.) Kiss her neck, her shoulders, pull her top down over her shoulder to kiss her shoulders, its sexy and she'll like it. Lift her top up to kiss her stomach. Move all over her body kiss her legs, her thighs, kiss her shins and her feet. Roll her over and kiss the back of her neck, her back, her buttocks, her legs, etc.

3) Now begin to undress her as you kiss her. Open her blouse and kiss her all over her chest and her stomach, kiss her on her bra, pull her bra strap off her shoulder and kiss her shoulders, pull her bra down a little and kiss the top of her breasts, pull it down a little more and lick her nipples, pop her breasts out o her bra cup and such her nipples. After a while place her breast back in her bra and move to another spot. If she is wearing pants undue her zipper, pull her pants open slightly around the zipper and kiss her around her waistline and her pubic area. Kiss her legs with her pants on, kiss her between the legs with her pants on. If she is wearing a dress or a skirt, lift her skirt up and kiss her legs and thighs, kiss her waistline and her pubic area, kiss her between her legs. - Then move down to her feet kissing every part of her body all the while.

4) Flip her over. Kiss the back of her neck, lift her shirt up and kiss her back. Now undue her bra and kiss her back some more. Kiss her butt with her panties on. After a while, if she is wearing pants now it is time to take them off. Roll her over, and pull them off of her. If she is wearing a skirt take her panties off, but leave her skirt on. Now it is time to start giving her some oral sex. Reach and

withdraw. Give her some oral sex, then go back to some French kissing, now humping her with your body as you kiss her. Kiss and suck on her breasts again. If she has multiple orgasms now is the time to give her, her first orgasm. Give her oral sex while using your finger to massage her g-spot at the same time. If she is a single orgasm woman, turn her on with oral sex, but withdraw before she comes.

5) Now it is time to take all her clothes off and remove yours. Make sure she is still wet, go back to French kissing and kissing her all over her body while playing with her vagina and clitoris with your finger. Suck her breasts again. Lick her breasts and her stomach - Make sure her vagina is soaking wet before you enter. Now it is time to enter. (I won't go into positions - see " Everything You Ever Wanted To Know About Sex Positions" and the "Kama Sutra" on or web site for that - as positions will be varied from time to time depending on our mood and the girl - different people fit better in different ways.)

6) Enter slowly, caress her close to you, hug her, hold her. Do not enter all the way at first. Use short slow strokes and only insert an inch or so then withdraw. Set up a rhythm. Slowly enter deeper, working your way up to full deep thrusts over time.

7) Pay attention to her body signals. Women come in different ways. Some get tight and hard all over when they are getting ready to come. Others get aggressive and change into a position that is easy for them to come in with you. Other get vocal, others start sweating. Everyone is different. Know your woman and know her signals.

8) Know your timing. Are you trying to make love for hours or all night, or all you trying to give each of you an orgasm and then end your session. Or are you trying to give her (or both of you) multiple orgasms and then call it a night. If intending to go a long time or all night, reach and withdraw from the orgasm point, so as to not quite have an orgasm until you are ready to end. If you are trying to give her (or you) multiple orgasms then depending on how she has her multiple orgasms you may need to simply keep yourself from coming until she has her orgasms. (See " How To Make Sex Last Longer") or you may give her (or you) an orgasm then withdraw from sex for a while talking or playing while hugging or caressing until ready to start again. Or you may simply revert to After Play until she is wet and you are hard again (See After Play below).

9) After Play - Don't end your love making on an orgasm. Follow through. Show her you love her and it is not just about sex and orgasms. Wind down with some foreplay which is now called after play. Kissing, hugging, kissing all over, touching, caressing, kissing. End with kissing. If you are working on multiple orgasms, after play can turn into foreplay and set you up for another love-making session. But even after multiple orgasms and multiple love-making sessions you will always end the whole thing with after play.

That is a sample of how to make love to a woman. Of course, it is done spontaneously. It is not to be memorized like a zombie or done exactly the same each time. In order to keep a relationship fresh, you have to avoid routine and habit and try new and varied techniques. But the things each of your love making sessions should always have in common are:

1) Sensuality
2) Lots of foreplay and after play
3) Use your whole body and make love to your partners whole body.
4) Lots of kissing.
5) Observation - get to know your partners body and how it works.
6) Communicate - talk to her as you make love. Say sweat nothings as well as finding out what feels good and what doesn't. (Also talk to her about sex, when you are not having sex. It is pre-session foreplay and it is a way of finding out what is needed or wanted,

Tantric Sex and Kama Sutra

If you want to be a good lover, Tantric sex technique is a good thing to learn. Some people think that Tantra has something to do with the Kama Sutra but it doesn't.

Let's clear up the confusion.

The Kama Sutra is Indian in origin. It has been translated into English a number of times by various people. The most widely known translation is by Sir Richard Burton in 1883.

The Kama Sutra was written by a celibate scholar. The Kama Sutra revolves around a man's pleasure. Did you know that only about 20% of the book is about sexual positioning?

Most people believe the Kama Sutra is a book about sexual positions.

It is way more extensive that that. The Kama Sutra is a comprehensive way of looking at sexuality. It is about getting to a place where you can maintain a good loving relationship, where sex is about pleasing each other and knowing how to make each other feel good.

The Kama Sutra is a great way for couples to keep their sex fun and fresh over the long term. I recommend it. The Kama Sutra has 36 chapters and 64 sex positions. It is not a quick read. And not everything it will pertain to all people. But it can keep you and your partner entertained for a lifetime. You can get a copy of the full text of the original Sir Richard Burton translation of the Kama Sutra here: http://datingtorelating.com/ebooks on our website.

Modern Tantra sexual practices, on the other hand, have evolved from classic Hindu and Buddhist Tantra which would take years to learn and require a master to teach you, and is way more extensive then just sexual practices. Traditional Tantra is a way of channeling the energy of god or the universe within all of us.

Tantra Sex as practiced today prolongs the act of lovemaking and focuses on channeling potent orgasmic energies moving through you thereby raising your consciousness.

Tantra can help you with control to make sex last longer for both you and your partner, it can help you achieve more intense orgasms, multiple orgasms (for both men and women) and with a partner who is also into Tantra you can take sex into a spiritual level of closeness and consciousness that is not usually found.

To help achieve this the man needs to have proper ejaculatory control and the woman needs to have control over her vagina and womb. Both partners need to have proper breath control.

For a free eBook giving you some Tantra exercises and techniques go to our website: http://datingtorelating.com/tantricsex to download a copy.

Now for both the Kama Sutra and Tantra practices it is good to have a co-operative partner to learn and develop the techniques with. So as you start applying some of the principles I have discussed earlier in this book and have made sex a little more pleasurable for your wife or girlfriend, then moving into learning Tantra and Kama Sutra would definitely be a way to take your love life with your mate to the next level of pleasure for both of you.

Tantra training, however, is something that men can do singularly without their partner's co-operation or knowledge as a way to learn to enhance their partner's pleasure. Learning how to control your ejaculation, for example, can lead to longer sex and the ability to make sure your partner comes first.

So learning some of these Tantra techniques is something that you may want to start (before you have your partner's co-operation) in your quest to get your wife or girlfriend to want more sex. I suggest that you read the free eBook and apply some of the techniques.

Now here is a little Tantra technique that was taught to me 30 years ago by women. I didn't even know it was Tantra until five years ago or so when I was looking up some Tantra techniques on line and found it described on a Tantra website. I've been using this technique for years to double the intensity of a woman's orgasm. Believe me, it works and you can use it on women who don't know anything about Tantra.

THE TRIPLE WHAMMY

I call it the TRIPLE WHAMMY! It works like this:

So while giving your partner oral sex with your lips and tongue, begin massaging the lips of her vagina with your index finger. When she opens up begin inserting your index finger into her vagina. Work your finger like a penis. Slowly inserting and withdrawing as needed until she is soaking wet internally. If you know how to find the g-spot begin massaging that also while working your finger in and out. (If you don't know how to find the G-spot get a copy of our free eReport "How To Find A Woman's G-spot" here: http://datingtorelating.com/howtofindawomansgspot)

Keep working and exciting her clit with your tongue or thumb (when and if you withdraw your mouth from her vagina. It can be done either way while your index finger is inserted into her vagina.) When she is very wet, excited and totally into it, begin massaging her anus opening lightly with your middle finger. If you do it right the anus will act like a vagina and begin to open up just as the vagina does when you lightly massage it.

As it opens up begin inserting – only as deep as the opening allows - your middle finger (this is important as it can hurt slightly if you try to force your finger up the anus just as it would hurt if you try to force your finger into a vagina). The anus is a sexual organ and will become lubricated as does the vagina. As it gets excited, it will open up more and more allowing for deeper penetration. Work your middle finger in an out in unison with your index finger which is inserted into the vagina and working in and out like a penis, all the while messaging the clit with your tongue or thumb.

By the time she is ready to come the anus should be all the way open and allow your middle finger to move in and out fully in unison with your index finger.

THIS IS A TRIPLE WHAMMY FOR THE GIRL. She will have a clitoral, vaginal, and anal orgasm ALL AT ONCE. In addition, if you know how to locate her G-spot and massage it while doing the other, you will give her a QUADRUPLE WHAMMY – clitoral, vaginal, g-spot, and anal orgasms all at once.

Guys should be so lucky! (Girls can do a similar technique on a guy, by the way, with just one finger in his anus working as described above while giving him oral sex. This is a DOUBLE WHAMMY and intensifies an orgasm for a guy!)

Now when you learn to give a woman the TRIPLE/QUADRUPLE WHAMMY and do it right, she will want sex a lot – I guarantee you – unless you are really not doing your job as a man in other areas. But ordinarily even if you are messing up in other areas – she will still want lots of sex from you. She may even divorce you and still have sex with you for a while after that until she gets another partner. THAT is how powerful the TRIPLE/QUADRUPLE WHAMMY is when you master it.

Now some women aren't into anal sex and will resist you doing this to them if you talk about it or bring it up. Usually this happens on first date type sex or new relationships. If you have been with a woman for a while, you will already know if she has a thing for or against anal sex. Now this is not the same as sticking a penis up a woman's anus. This is what people think of as the usual traditional anal sex. A finger is a lot smaller than a penis, and is a lot easier way to create pleasure and orgasm through the anus than a penis.

Now some women don't resist it because of the thought of the size of the instrument being stuck up their anus, they resist it because they have considerations about the anus being dirty and they would feel embarrassed if you got their feces on your finger while doing this.

If you turn on the anus properly with massage and let it open up naturally on its own, this should not happen. The anus IS a sexual organ and I have even seen "cum" come out of a woman's anus. It is a white milky substance that comes out as she is turned on and as she is coming.

Now with new partners I usually do not talk about this or ask permission. If you do it right and she is turned on, she will not even notice what you are doing exactly and/or won't care. After it is all over and she experienced the TRIPLE ORGASM, she might ask out of curiosity "Did you stick one of your fingers up my anus?"

Of course when she asks I tell her yes. However, after she experiences the pleasure I have never had any woman say, "Don't do that again."

Now with a few women they will be super aware and will resist you even massaging the anus. So with those women you might have to talk about it (some other time when not having sex) and explain to her that it creates an intensified orgasm. Handle her considerations about cleanliness by having her (and you) take a shower or bath right before sex, and perhaps going to the bathroom to empty the bowels before the shower.

If all of that fails then it is her loss and not yours so do not worry about it, Just do the DOUBLE WHAMMY which is oral or thumb massaging the clit while inserting the finger into her vagina and massaging the g-spot.

Perhaps you can wait a couple of years until sexual routines start getting boring and try again.

After Play – A Little Known Secret

Relationships aren't all about sex. And one of the ways to get more sex is to let a woman know it is not all about sex for you.

The typical young man has sex with his girl, doesn't make her come, then falls asleep on top of her after he comes. (See why a woman might not want to have a lot of sex with this type of guy?)

One of the ways to let a woman know it is not all about sex for you is "After Play." I never hear many people write about after play. Nor do I even hear women talk about after play very much. For them the complaints are usually guys not doing enough foreplay.

But after play is a VERY important topic if you want to get more sex out of your wife or girlfriend.

I talked about after play above when I gave a sample of how to make love to a woman. But here it is again.

After Play - Don't end your love making on an orgasm. Follow through. Show her you love her and it is not just about sex and orgasms. Wind down with some foreplay which is now called after play. Kissing, hugging, kissing all over, touching, caressing, kissing. End with kissing. If you are working on multiple orgasms, after play can turn into foreplay and set you up for another lovemaking session. But even after multiple orgasms and multiple lovemaking sessions you will always end the whole thing with after play.

Personally I like to do lots of kissing and kiss a woman all over her body as my final after play.

ABOUT THE AUTHOR

Mr. L. Rx is the author of the Dating To Relating website (www.DatingToRelating.com – a popular "dating tip" site for men with over 500,000 unique visitors per month) and the author of the eReport "How I Got 700 Dates In One Year." And the newest eBook "How To Get Your Wife Or Girlfriend To Want More Sex" (all available at http://www.datingtorelating.com)

In his fifties, Mr. L. Rx has some times been called the "Observational Guru" rather than a "Dating Guru" as it is his ability to observe throughout his fifty plus years of experience that allows him to share dozens of unique dating and relationship strategies that apply to different personality types and different situations.

Unlike other "Gurus" who give you one strategy that works for them and then apply it to "all men or women," Mr. L. Rx acknowledges that people have different personalities and that different personalities require different strategies.

Mr. L. Rx's techniques and strategies work for any man no matter what he looks like. Mr. L. Rx points out that he personally has had thousands of dates with beautiful young women in his forties and fifties whereas in his teen years and early twenties when he was a hot-looking young man in his prime, he couldn't get a date.

Mr. L. Rx teaches men and women his unique "observational technology" which allows you to develop your own situationally correct strategies for your own situation and personality in addition to Mr. L. Rx giving you dozens of already tried and proven techniques of his own.

Mr. L. Rx believes that successful relationships develop from sane dating habits and technique, and that communication, observation, and create are the foundations of a successful relationship.

Mr. L. Rx is a firm champion of monogamy when in a committed relationship and a firm believer in "multiple dating" when not in a committed relationship.

Mr. L. Rx believes in family values and is the proud father of four children (three girls and a boy.)

Appendix A: Sex Training Books From Dating To Relating

How To Make Sex Last Longer - by Dr. Dating
Reg. Price: ~~$20.00~~
Sale Price: $7.00
Save: $13.00

SPECIAL OFFER

PayPal
Add To Cart

HOW TO MAKE SEX LAST LONGER   - $ 7.00

How To Make Sex Last Longer
Many sexually active males would like to "keep it up" longer - until their woman is fully satisfied and for their own more fulfilling, long lasting pleasure. Since it's no secret that it takes women longer to climax, guys need to delay their ejaculation if they really want to satisfy their partner. Everyone knows that longer intercourse is much more satisfying than "quickies" for both parties. Thanks to Dr. Dating, the secret is out - everyone can easily lengthen their lovemaking just by applying the techniques from Dr. Dating's latest eBook, *How to Make Sex Last Longer.*

** NEW 2007 Version **

Reg. Price: $20.00
Sale Price: $7.00
Save: $13.00

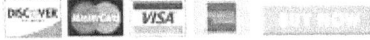

HOW TO GIVE ANY WOMAN ORGASMS - $7.00

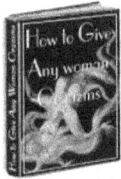

** NEW 2007 Version **

How To Give Any Woman Orgasms
The female body is a mystery to most men - even to those who have had thousands of sexual conquests. What is it that makes women tick? What do women really want in bed? These questions may have perplexed you for so long, and you're not alone. Finally, Dr. Dating has written a complete, tried and tested guide on *How to Give Any Woman Orgasms*.

Reg. Price: $100.00
Sale Price: $14.00
Save: $86.00

NEW ARRIVAL

PayPal
Add To Cart

SPECIAL OFFER!

Buy HOW TO MAKE SEX LAST LONGER and HOW TO GIVE ANY WOMAN ORGASMS - $14.00

and get THREE FREE compilation eBooks FROM Mr. L. Rx

EVERYTHING YOU WANTED TO KNOW ABOUT SEX POSITIONS

HOW TO BE A GREAT LOVER

HOW TO BE A GREAT KISSER

Appendix B: Other Books From Dating To Relating

How To Be Successful with Women - by Dr. Dating

Reg. Price: $20.00
Sale Price: $7.00
Save: $13.00

SPECIAL OFFER

DISCOVER MasterCard VISA

PayPal
Add To Cart

HOW TO BE SUCCESSFUL WITH WOMEN - $7.00

** NEW 2007 Version **

How To Be Successful With Women

Ever thrown your arms up in the air, confused about something a woman said or did? You're not alone! Most men don't have an answer to the question of "What do women want?" Most men, that is, except for Dr. Dating. In his eBook "How to Be Successful with Women," Dr. Dating tackles the complexities of the female mind, and he's written it for YOU! He's handing you nothing short of the keys to the kingdom.

Reg. Price: $20.00
Sale Price: $7.00
Save: $13.00

SPECIAL OFFER

DISCOVER MasterCard VISA [ ] BUY NOW

PayPal
Add To Cart

THE ART OF CONVERSATION - $ 7.00

** Published 2006 **

The Art Of Conversation

We've all been there - the non-stop sweating and stuttering slowly becomes an embarrassment because you're simply too nervous to talk to the object of your attraction. Whether you're a sensitive guy or a sassy girl, you probably still get tongue-tied during parties, first dates, or even a simple conversation in your office lounge. Not to worry - Dr. Dating has created just the thing that can help you get your tongue out of a twist.

Reg. Price: ~~$20.00~~
Sale Price: $7.00
Save: $13.00

SPECIAL OFFER

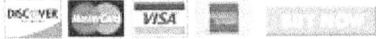

DISCOVER   MasterCard   VISA

PayPal
Add To Cart

THE BEGINNER'S GUIDE TO VIRTUAL SEX - $ 7.00

The Beginners Guide to Virtual Sex

It doesn't matter if you're a virgin or promiscuous, single or in a committed relationship - ABSOLUTELY ANYONE can have fulfilling, pleasurable sex in the virtual world. All you need is a phone line or an internet connection. This guide will show you EVERYTHING you need to know about mastering the world of virtual sex.

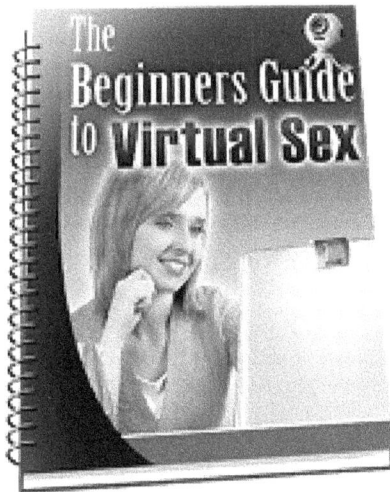

** Published 2007 **

Reg. Price: ~~$20.00~~
Sale Price: $7.00
Save: $13.00

SPECIAL OFFER

DISCOVER MasterCard VISA [American] BUY NOW

PayPal
Add To Cart

HOW TO FIND A F**K BUDDY - $7.00

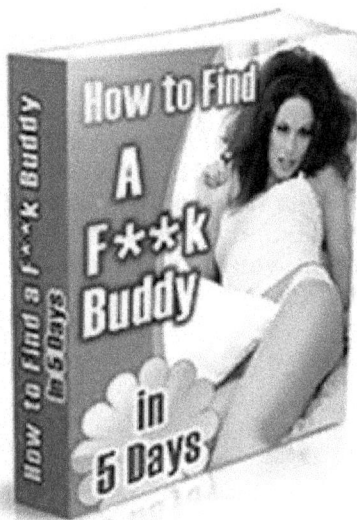

<u>How To Find A F**k Buddy</u>

If you think it's impossible to list "sex" as a recreational activity, you're wrong! Whether you're as suave as James Bond or as ordinary as the Average Joe, you need to know the secrets of finding your own special "friend with benefits". Having a fk buddy can be a sensual adventure unlike any other and you deserve to be on that adventure! This guide can give you tried and tested methods that will help you get the f**k buddy**

** Published 2007 **

Reg. Price: $20.00
Sale Price: $7.00
Save: $13.00

SPECIAL OFFER

DISCOVER MasterCard VISA ☐ BUY NOW

PayPal
Add To Cart

COPING WITH A SMALL PENIS - $7.00

Coping With A Small Penis
This eBook is an inspiring story about how a young man copes with a small penis - and uses this "lack of size" as an advantage. It's no secret that most men worry about whether they are "big enough" to please a woman, and this story will definitely make you feel better about the size of your own penis, as well as your masculinity.

** NEW 2007 Version **

Reg. Price: ~~$20.00~~
Sale Price: $7.00
Save: $13.00

SPECIAL OFFER

DISCOVER MasterCard VISA [   ] BUY NOW

PayPal
Add To Cart

DEALING WITH LONELINESS - $ 7.00

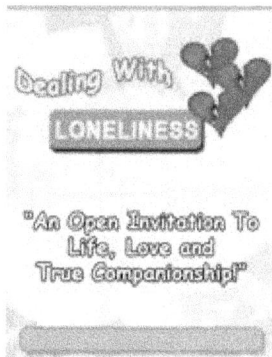

"An Open Invitation To
Life, Love and
True Companionship"

"Dealing With Loneliness"

By: SideKick

Dealing With Loneliness, while self explanatory, is one of the biggest problems for singles. This eBook is a quick and easy guide to tackling this problem and is a must read for all.

** Published 2007 **

Reg. Price: $20.00
Sale Price: $7.00
Save: $13.00

DISCOVER MasterCard VISA ____ BUY NOW

PayPal
Add To Cart

PERSONALITY TYPES AND DATING GUIDE- $ 7.00

"Personality Quadrant's Dating Guide"

By: SideKick

Personality Quadrant's Dating Guide is a fun-filled, light-hearted guide on how to get a good date by understanding yourself as well as understanding and interpreting how your date will behave based on his or her personality type!

** Published 2007 **

Reg. Price: $20.00
Sale Price: $7.00
Save: $13.00

SPECIAL OFFER

BUY NOW

PayPal
Add To Cart

GUIDE TO ADULT DATING - $ 7.00

Guide To Adult Dating

If you're tired of the normal dating routines of going out for coffee or dinner with someone you just met in a bar, you might want to try a *spicier* style of dating. Adult dating may just be the thing to kick your sex life into high gear. It's for anyone who wants to explore the extent of their sexuality, bring their fantasies to life, or try something new. With Dr. Dating's "Guide to Adult Dating", you can venture into the highly coveted world of sexy adult dates.

** Published 2006 **

Reg. Price: $20.00
Sale Price: $7.00
Save: $13.00

SPECIAL OFFER

DISCOVER MasterCard VISA BUY NOW

PayPal
Add To Cart

GREAT TIPS FOR DATING SUCCESS - $ 7.00

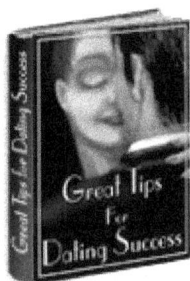

Great Tips For Dating Success

Whether you're looking for a fun, casual dating experience or a powerful romantic encounter, Dr. Dating's *Great Tips for Dating Success* is just the guide you need. This guide was written and researched by Dr. Dating himself, to help people form all walks of life to find and enjoy great dates. This eBook has all the hot tips and tricks that will help increase your dating success.

** NEW 2007 Version **

Reg. Price: $20.00
Sale Price: $7.00
Save: $13.00

SPECIAL OFFER

DISCOVER MasterCard VISA   BUY NOW

PayPal
Add To Cart

5 STEPS TO ONLINE DATING SUCCESS - $ 7.00

5 Steps To Online Dating Success -

By: SideKick

-What You Need to Know About Online Dating First!
-What Makes Online Dating So Different?
-Getting Started
-Making Yourself Look Like A Million Dollars

** Published 2007 **

Reg. Price: $20.00
Sale Price: $7.00
Save: $13.00

SPECIAL OFFER

DISCOVER MasterCard VISA

PayPal
Add To Cart

GUIDE TO ONLINE DATING - $ 7.00

** NEW 2007 Version **

Guide To Online Dating

Be honest - the single life can be depressing sometimes. You may try to find dates in bars, ask your friends to hook you up with someone, or even try dating services. If you don't' seem to have any success, you might find yourself giving up. But there's probably one dating frontier you haven't tried - online dating. More and more people all over the world are increasing their dating chances through the opportunities offered on the internet. With Dr. Dating's *Guide to Online Dating*, you can use the internet to give your dating life a complete makeover!

Reg. Price: $20.00
Sale Price: $7.00
Save: $13.00

SPECIAL OFFER

DISCOVER MasterCard VISA [ ] BUY NOW

PayPal
Add To Cart

THE ULTIMATE MAN'S GUIDE TO ONLINE DATING - $ 7.00

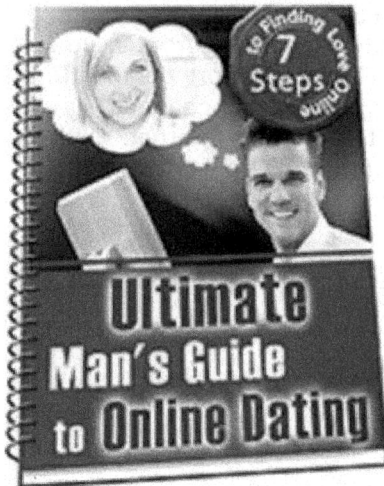

The Ultimate Man's Guide to Online Dating

Ever feel like you're meeting the wrong women? Have you dated around and found that you're looking for something more casual while your date wants a marriage? Or do you simply get nervous in front of an attractive girl? Trust me, we've all been there. Sometimes we'd rather hang out with the guys and watch a football game rather than risk the frustration of going out with women you don't want to see again. There's a better world of women out there - and Dr. Dating has written the perfect dating guide for you!

** Published 2007 **

Reg. Price: ~~$20.00~~
Sale Price: $7.00
Save: $13.00

SUCCESSFUL ONLINE DATING - UK EDITION - $ 7.00

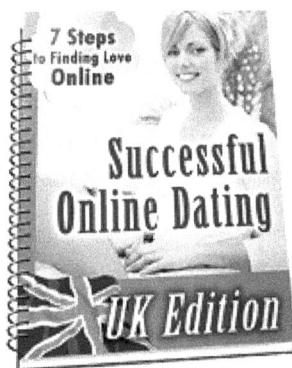

Successful Online Dating - UK Edition

Face it, mate - the dating world can be scary. When you think about dating, you think about the stress, rejection, and anxiety that comes with it. Why even date at all? The good news is that ONLINE DATING has changed all this. We now live in a world where we can collect and select potential dates without the grueling experiences of real world dating. By the time you actually meet an online date in person, you're ready for it! You know who you're dealing with. You know you won't face rejection ever again.

** Published 2007 **

Reg. Price: $20.00
Sale Price: $7.00
Save: $13.00

SPECIAL OFFER

DISCOVER MasterCard VISA [card] BUY NOW

PayPal
Add To Cart

A TEENAGER'S GUIDE TO DATING - $ 7.00

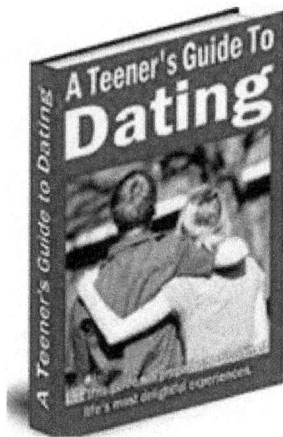

"A Teenager's Guide To Dating"

By: SideKick

This is a comprehensive 128 page eBook written for Teenagers and the Adults who care about them. This eBook covers every aspect of teenage dating. A must for Teenagers and their Parents alike.

** Published 2007 **

Reg. Price: $20.00
Sale Price: $7.00
Save: $13.00

SPECIAL OFFER

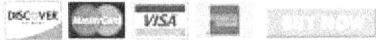

DISCOVER MasterCard VISA

PayPal
Add To Cart

SUCCESSFUL DATING FOR WOMEN - $ 7.00

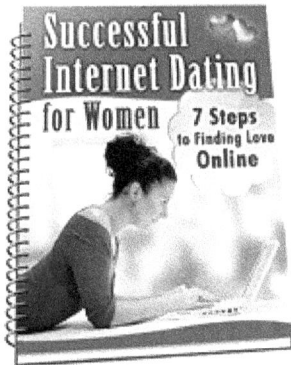

Successful Internet Dating For Women

Ever feel like you're *never* going to find the man of your dreams? Have you dated around and found most of your dates frustrating and disappointing? Trust me, girl, we've all been there. Sometimes we'd rather sit on the couch, eat some ice cream, and watch the latest John Cusack movie. *There has to be a better life than this, right?* Well, there is! We've got the ultimate dating guide to help you find Mr. Right!

** Published 2007 **

Reg. Price: ~~$20.00~~
Sale Price: $7.00
Save: $13.00

SPECIAL OFFER

DISCOVER MasterCard VISA [card] BUY NOW

PayPal
Add To Cart

"How I got over 700 dates in one year (and 2500 women's phone numbers)" - $7.00

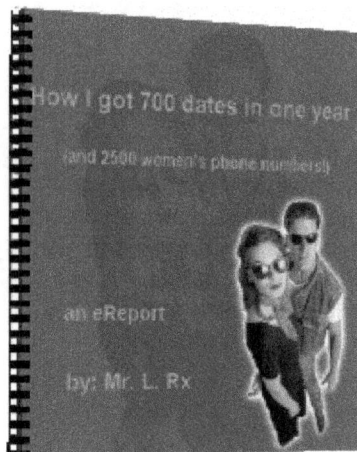

Why settle for doubling your dating when you can 10 x it!

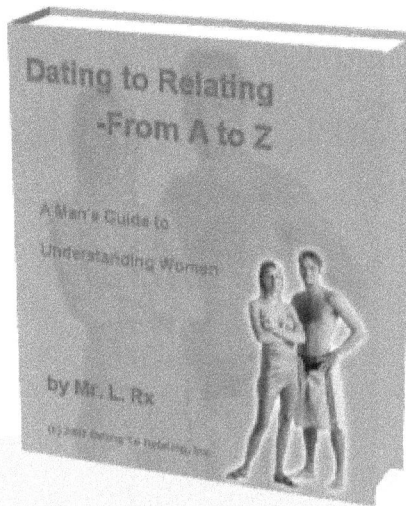

Dating To Relating - The Book
Price:$39.95

Dating to Relating - from A to Z (A man's guide to Understanding women)

"How I went from Stupid to Smart in just 50 years" or

"How and Why I got more dates with, relationships with and proposals from Hot Young Woman at age 50 than I did at age 25.

www.ingramcontent.com/pod-product-compliance
Lightning Source LLC
Chambersburg PA
CBHW080621270326
41928CB00016B/3150